My Very First Look at
Colours

LONDON · PRINCETON

www.two-canpublishing.com

Published by Two-Can Publishing,
43–45 Dorset Street, London W1U 7NA

© Two-Can Publishing 2001

For information on Two-Can books and multimedia,
call (0)20 7224 2440, fax (0)20 7224 7005, or visit our
website at http://www.two-canpublishing.com

Conceived, designed and edited by

Picthall & Gunzi Ltd

21A Widmore Road, Bromley, Kent BR1 1RW

Original concept: Chez Picthall
Editor: Lauren Robertson
Designer: Dominic Zwemmer
Photography: Steve Gorton
Additional photographs: Daniel Pangbourne
DTP: Tony Cutting, Ray Bryant
Cover design: Paul Calver

'Two-Can' is a trademark of Two-Can Publishing.
Two-Can Publishing is a division of Zenith Entertainment Ltd,
43–45 Dorset Street, London W1U 7NA.

ISBN 1–85434–939–2

2 4 6 8 10 9 7 5 3 1

A catalogue record for this book is available from the British Library.

Colour reproduction by Next Century Ltd.
Printed in Italy.

My Very First Look at
Colours

Christiane Gunzi

LONDON · PRINCETON

Red

toothbrush

tomato

scissors

shoes

raspberries

cotton

How many shoes can you see?

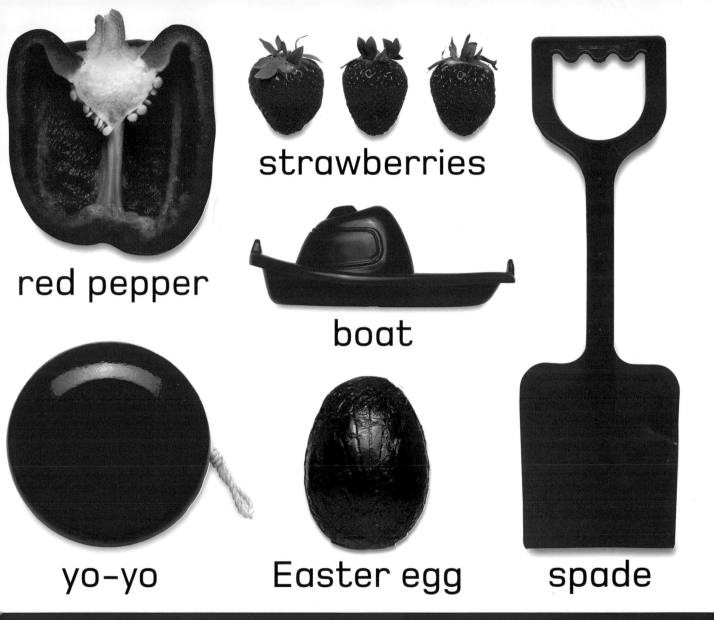

red pepper

strawberries

boat

yo-yo

Easter egg

spade

Can you find the toothbrush?

Orange

marigold

egg cup

T-shirt

sweets

apricots

ball of wool

How many apricots can you see?

carrots

saucepan

lentils

buttons

beaker

shell

orange

What things here can you eat?

Yellow

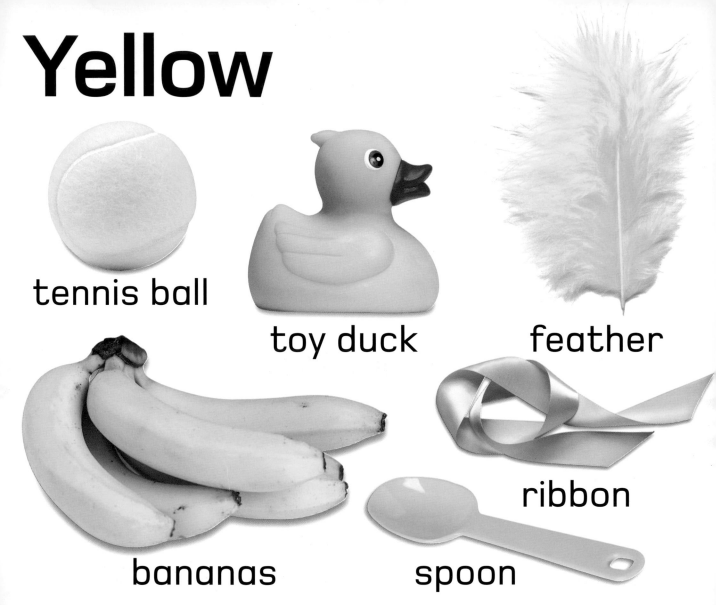

tennis ball

toy duck

feather

bananas

spoon

ribbon

Which bird has yellow feathers?

bricks

cheese

ice lolly

sunflower

lemon

balloon

Which things are square?

Green

candle

pasta

socks

peas

leaf

grapes

Can you find the curly pasta?

comb

crayon

apple

ball

mug

boots

Is there anything here to eat?

Blue

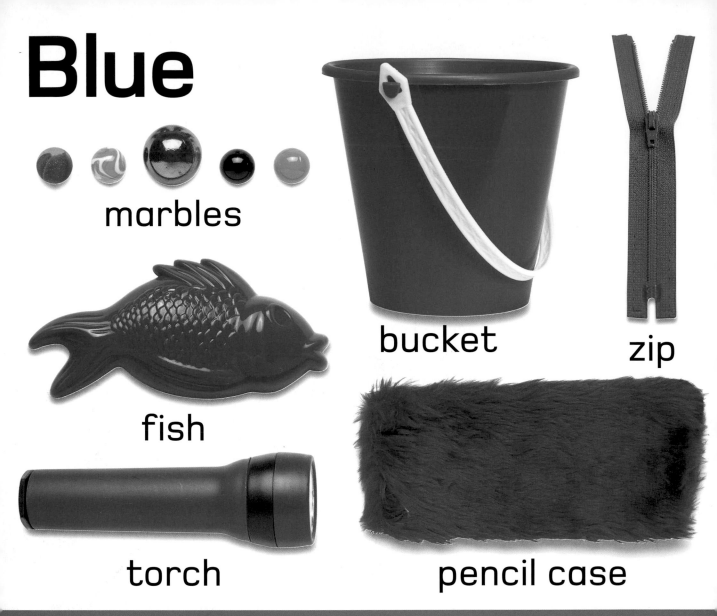

marbles

bucket

zip

fish

torch

pencil case

What can you put water in?

toy car

blueberries

paper clips

candles

jeans

fork

What do you eat your food with?

Pink

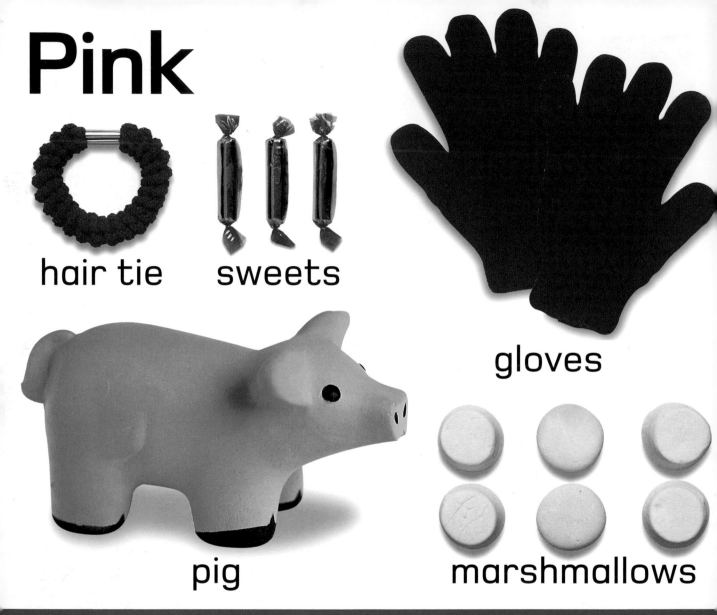

hair tie

sweets

gloves

pig

marshmallows

What farm animal can you see?

cake

handbag

magic wand

pencils

yogurt

prawns

soap

Which do you use for washing?

Purple

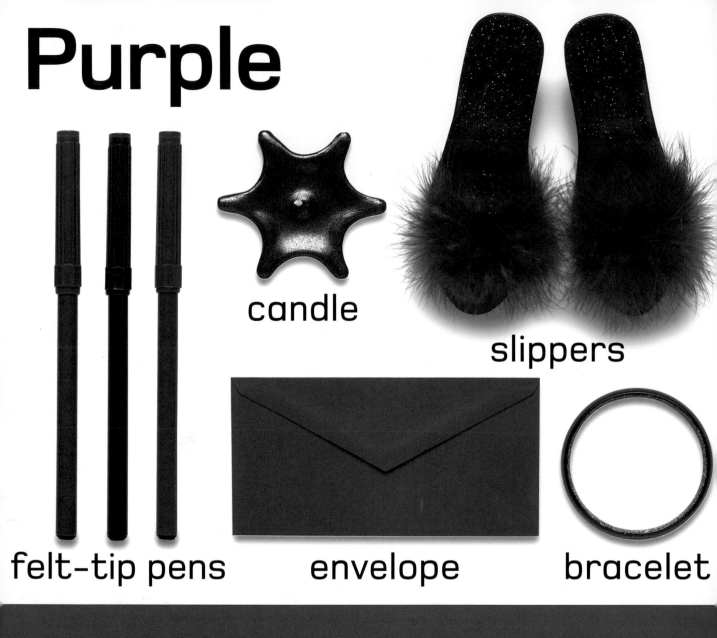

candle

slippers

felt-tip pens

envelope

bracelet

What things here can you wear?

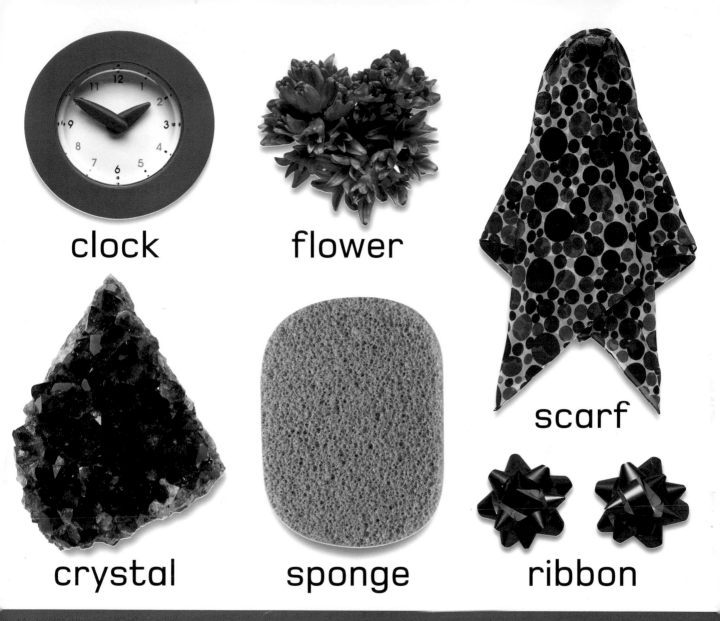

clock

flower

scarf

crystal

sponge

ribbon

What helps you to tell the time?

Brown

chocolates

onion

biscuits

gingerbread

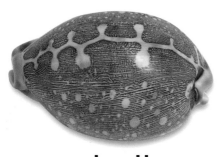
shell

fir cone

What shape are the chocolates?

Grey

tin can

mouse

school socks

bow tie

elephant

pencils

Which picture is your favourite?

Gold

stars

ring

mask

heart

chocolate coins

sun

sweets

Can you count the gold coins?

Silver

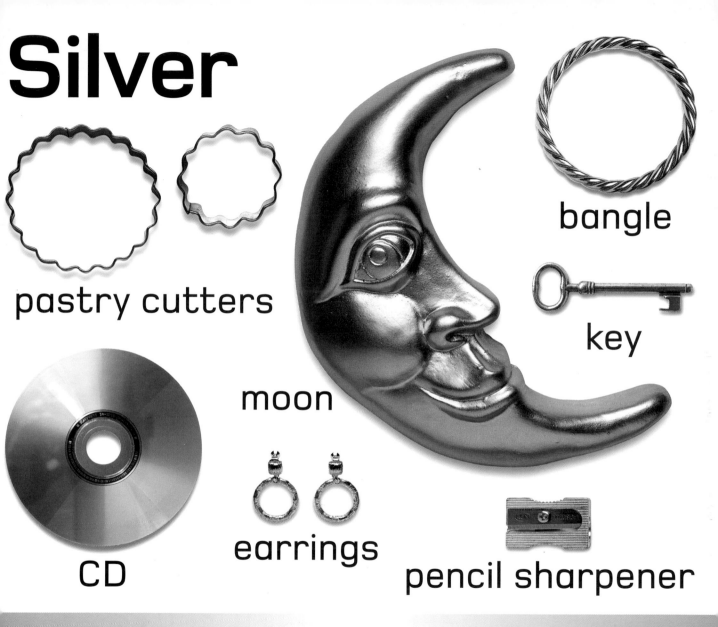

pastry cutters

bangle

key

moon

CD

earrings

pencil sharpener

Can you count the round things?

Black

toy car

ink

shoes

coal

cat

olives

Is there a friendly pet here?

White

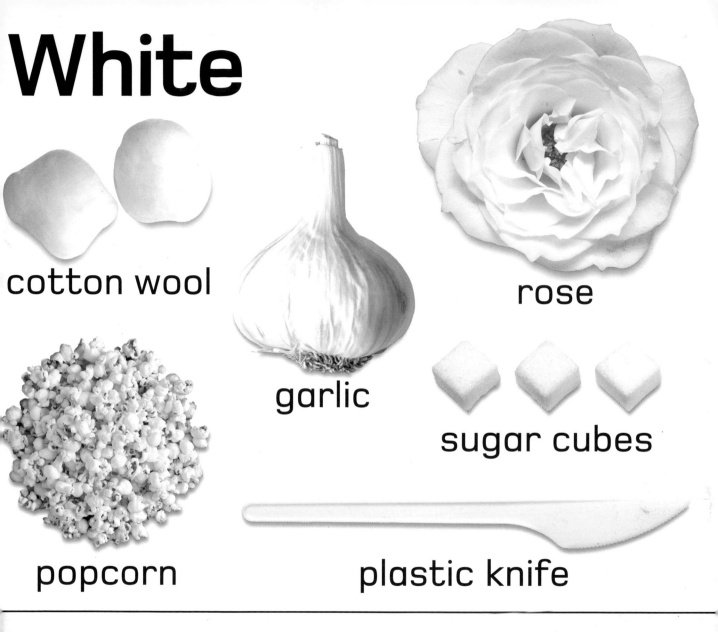

cotton wool

garlic

rose

sugar cubes

popcorn

plastic knife

Is there something soft here?

What colour?

sweets

ink

marigold

cotton

crayon

candle

toy duck

How many colours can you see?